HAL·LEONARD

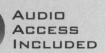
WEDDING
ESSENTIALS

AUDIO
ACCESS
INCLUDED

PLAYBACK+
Speed · Pitch · Balance · Loop

WEDDING TRUMPET SOLOS

To access audio visit:
www.halleonard.com/mylibrary

Enter Code
3445-1203-6300-7249

ISBN 978-1-4234-9921-3

HAL·LEONARD®
CORPORATION
7777 W. BLUEMOUND RD. P.O. BOX 13819 MILWAUKEE, WI 53213

In Australia Contact:
Hal Leonard Australia Pty. Ltd.
4 Lentara Court
Cheltenham, Victoria, 3192 Australia
Email: ausadmin@halleonard.com.au

Visit Hal Leonard Online at
www.halleonard.com

AIR ON THE G STRING

from ORCHESTRAL SUITE NO. 3

By JOHANN SEBASTIAN BACH

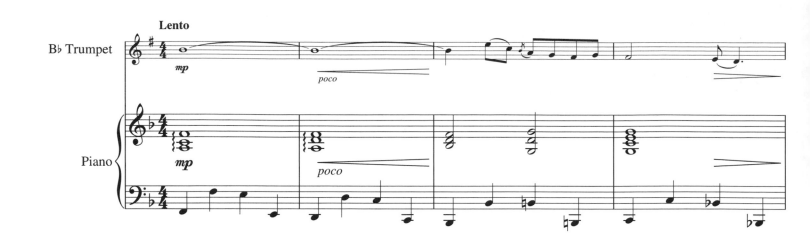

ALLEGRO MAESTOSO
from WATER MUSIC

By GEORGE FRIDERIC HANDEL

AVE MARIA

By FRANZ SCHUBERT

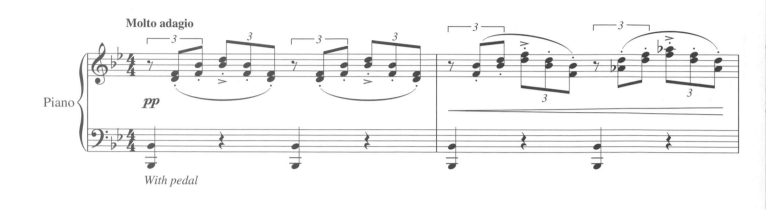

JUPITER
(Chorale Theme)
from THE PLANETS

By GUSTAV HOLST

RONDEAU

By JEAN-JOSEPH MOURET

TRIUMPHAL MARCH
from AÏDA

By GIUSEPPE VERDI

HAL•LEONARD

AUDIO
ACCESS
INCLUDED

PLAYBACK+
Speed • Pitch • Balance • Loop

WEDDING
TRUMPET SOLOS

HAL•LEONARD® CORPORATION

7777 W. BLUEMOUND RD. P.O. BOX 13819 MILWAUKEE, WI 53213

HL00842500

AIR ON THE G STRING

from ORCHESTRAL SUITE NO. 3

By JOHANN SEBASTIAN BACH

B♭ Trumpet

ALLEGRO MAESTOSO
from WATER MUSIC

B♭ Trumpet

By GEORGE FRIDERIC HANDEL

AVE MARIA

B♭ Trumpet

By FRANZ SCHUBERT

JUPITER
(Chorale Theme)
from THE PLANETS

By GUSTAV HOLST

B♭ Trumpet

ODE TO JOY

from SYMPHONY NO. 9 IN D MINOR, FOURTH MOVEMENT CHORAL THEME

Words by HENRY VAN DYKE
Music by LUDWIG VAN BEETHOVEN

B♭ Trumpet

RONDEAU

B♭ Trumpet

By JEAN-JOSEPH MOURET

TRIUMPHAL MARCH
from AÏDA

B♭ Trumpet

By GIUSEPPE VERDI

TRUMPET TUNE

Bb Trumpet

By HENRY PURCELL

WEDDING MARCH
from A MIDSUMMER NIGHT'S DREAM

Bb Trumpet

By FELIX MENDELSSOHN

TRUMPET VOLUNTARY

B♭ Trumpet

By JEREMIAH CLARKE

TRUMPET TUNE

By HENRY PURCELL

TRUMPET VOLUNTARY

By JEREMIAH CLARKE

WEDDING MARCH
from A MIDSUMMER NIGHT'S DREAM

By FELIX MENDELSSOHN

ODE TO JOY
from SYMPHONY NO. 9 IN D MINOR, FOURTH MOVEMENT CHORAL THEME

Words by HENRY VAN DYKE
Music by LUDWIG VAN BEETHOVEN